THE TAYLOR SWIFT EFFECT

FROM FASHION TO FOOTBALL

BY JENNA TOLLI

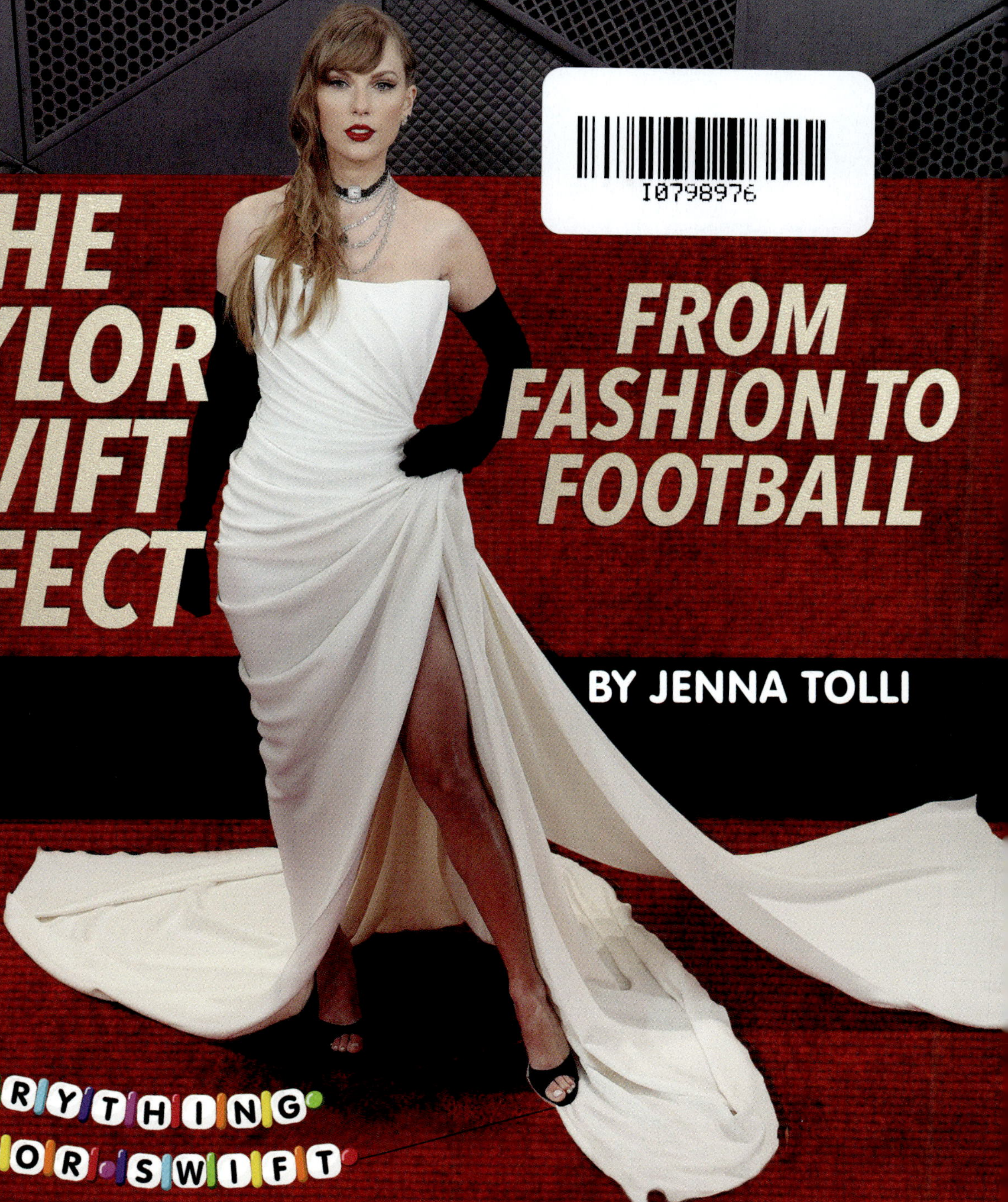

EVERYTHING TAYLOR SWIFT

(Gareth's Version)

Gareth Stevens PUBLISHING

Please visit our website, www.garethstevens.com. For a free color catalog of all our high-quality books, call toll free 1-800-542-2595 or fax 1-877-542-2596.

Library of Congress Cataloging-in-Publication Data
Names: Tolli, Jenna, author.
Title: The Taylor Swift effect : from fashion to football / Jenna Tolli.
Description: Buffalo, New York : Gareth Stevens Publishing, 2025. | Series: Everything Taylor Swift (Gareth's version) | Includes index.
Identifiers: LCCN 2024031875 | ISBN 9781482469516 (library binding) | ISBN 9781482469509 (paperback) | ISBN 9781482469523 (ebook)
Subjects: LCSH: Swift, Taylor, 1989–Influence–Juvenile literature.
Classification: LCC ML3930.S989 T655 2025 | DDC 782.42164092–dc23/eng/20240719
LC record available at https://lccn.loc.gov/2024031875

Published in 2025 by
Gareth Stevens Publishing
2544 Clinton Street
Buffalo, NY 14224

Designer: Tanya Dellaccio Keeney
Editor: Kristen Rajczak Nelson

Photo credits: Cover (friendship bracelet) Yuliqwiart/Shutterstock.com; series background Shubchynska Iryna/Shutterstock.com; cover Sipa USA/Alamy Images; p. 5 (Fearless album) Patti McConville/Alamy Images; p. 5 (Midnights album) Hazel Plater/Shutterstock.com; pp. 5 (Folklore album), 6 Catrina Haze/Shutterstock.com; pp. 5 (1989 album), 11 (RED cd) Stefano Chiacchiarini '74/Shutterstock.com; p. 7 (main) A.PAES/Shutterstock.com; p. 9 (main) Chris Pizzello/Invision/AP Images; pp. 9 (inset), 13 Tinseltown/Shutterstock.com; p. 11 (1989 vinyl), John Hanson Pye/Shutterstock.com; p. 15 PA Images/Alamy Images; p. 17 (top left) s_bukley/Shutterstock; p. 17 (top right) Dfree/Shutterstock.com; p. 17 (bottom left) Ovidiu Hrubaru/Shutterstock.com; p. 17 (bottom right) https://upload.wikimedia.org/wikipedia/commons/f/f9/Taylor_Swift_at_the_2024_Golden_Globes_%283%29.png; p. 19 Courtesy of Michael Hicks/Flickr.com; pp. 21 (inset), 23 (1989 CDs) ChristinaAiko Photography/Shutterstock.com; p. 21 (main) Sarunyu L/Shutterstock.com; p. 23 (1989 vinyl) Steve Travelguide/Shutterstock.com; p. 25 Ed Zurga/FR34145 AP/AP Images; p. 27 Waqas 302/Shutterstock.com; p. 28 Everett Collection/Shutterstock.com; p. 29 Courtesy of Paolo Villanueva/Flickr.com.

Printed in the United States of America

CPSIA compliance information: Batch #CWGS25: For further information contact Gareth Stevens at 1-800-542-2595.

CONTENTS

BOLDFACE WORDS APPEAR IN THE GLOSSARY.

WHAT IS THE TAYLOR SWIFT EFFECT?

Taylor Swift is known all around the world for her music. She has lots of faithful fans, called Swifties, who have been greatly **impacted** by her songwriting.

But it's not only Taylor's music that impacts others. What she loves, what she speaks about, and ideas she cares about do too. Taylor's mark on so many different areas of popular culture, from music and fashion to **politics** and football, has been called the "Taylor Swift Effect."

KNOW IT ALL

Taylor is a big part of pop, or popular, culture! Pop culture includes all the things people talk about in everyday life such as music, movies, and famous people.

Taylor is a force in the music business. As of 2024, she's the only artist to win album of the year at the Grammy's four times!

folklore
won album of the year in 2021

Fearless
won album of the year in 2010

Midnights
won album of the year in 2024

1989
won album of the year in 2016

COUNTRY START

Taylor has been playing guitar since she was 12 years old! She's been writing songs for a long time too. At first, Taylor made country music, including her first two albums *Taylor Swift* (2006) and *Fearless* (2008). Even though her music later crossed over into pop, she had a big impact on the country **genre**.

In 2017, singer and songwriter Kelsea Ballerini told *Cosmopolitan* that Taylor "completely changed the music industry." She said: "I really think that she blazed a trail for all my fellow new women in country."

Taylor often writes about her experiences, or what has happened in her life. Fans feel like her songs apply to what they are going through too!

AN INSPIRATION

Taylor has inspired many people—especially girls—to learn to play guitar. Many artists also have said Taylor inspired them, including Maisie Peters, Gracie Abrams, Olivia Rodrigo, Phoebe Bridgers, and many more.

Taylor can make an impact on music just by talking about other artists too. She sings about singer Charlie Puth and the band The Starting Line in songs on her album *The Tortured Poets Department* (2024). Their music was **streamed** thousands more times shortly after the album came out, likely due to Taylor's shout outs.

PHOEBE BRIDGERS

In 2023, Phoebe Bridgers presented an award, or special prize, to Taylor and said, "I'm grateful to have grown up in a world with Taylor Swift in it, or, 'The World: Taylor's **Version**."

RIGHTS FOR MUSICIANS

Taylor has often used her fame to call attention to music artists' rights. She took her music off the streaming service Spotify from 2014 to 2017. She wanted music artists to be better paid when songs were streamed.

In 2020, Taylor's first record label, Big Machine Records, sold her **master recordings**. Because of this, she chose to rerecord the early albums she made with Big Machine. She wanted to own the masters of those songs. This made people talk more about artists' rights to own their music.

IN TAYLOR'S WORDS

"Music is art, and art is important and **rare**. Important, rare things are valuable. Valuable things should be paid for."
(*Wall Street Journal*, July 2014)

By October 2023, Taylor had rerecorded and released four of her six early albums. Each of her rerecorded album titles has "Taylor's Version" after it.

GETTING POLITICAL

Taylor shares her thoughts with her millions of followers on **social media**. When she says something, they want to know more!

In 2018, Taylor spoke out for the first time about politics. She wanted to support, or hold up and help, a political **candidate** from Tennessee who stood for equal rights for women and the **LGBTQ+** community. Within a few days of Taylor posting this on Instagram, over 100,000 people signed up to vote—especially young people. That's the Taylor Swift Effect in action!

In Taylor's speech at the American Music Awards in 2018, she reminded viewers to vote!

SAY IT IN A SONG

Taylor knows fans listen when she speaks—or sings. In the song "The Man" she sings: "I'm so sick of running as fast as I can / Wondering if I'd get there quicker if I was a man." It's about women being treated differently than men.

She also shows support for the LGBTQ+ community in "You Need to Calm Down." She sings: "Why are you mad? / When you could be GLAAD?" GLAAD is a group that supports LGBTQ+ rights, and her song drew positive attention to it.

Fans love that Taylor speaks out to support what she believes in! She won a 2019 MTV Video Music Award for "You Need to Calm Down"—which was decided by the fans.

SHE'LL NEVER GO OUT OF STYLE

Taylor's style has evolved, or changed, over time. Sometimes you can see a picture of Taylor and know which era, or time period, of her **career** it's from. When her first album came out, she wore a lot of cowboy boots and sundresses, for example!

Fans like to see what Taylor wears in her everyday life too. People say they like her clothes because they seem like something fans could wear too. Sometimes fans look for the same clothes or similar ones Taylor wore to buy for themselves!

KNOW IT ALL

Taylor is also known for her classic red lipstick, black eyeliner, and fun nail polish!

TAYLOR'S STYLE OVER THE YEARS

2008

2013

2016

2024

Fans enjoy recreating Taylor's famous outfits from different eras when they see her in concert!

IN TAYLOR'S WORDS

"For me, it's important to be comfortable in what I'm wearing."
(*ASOS*, January 2015)

THE ERAS TOUR

During 2023 and 2024, Taylor traveled the world on The Eras Tour. She played songs from all her past albums for thousands of fans.

So many people went to see The Eras Tour that cities hosting the concerts got an economic boost. This means people spent more money on hotels, going out to eat, and businesses in those cities than usual. When she played six sold-out shows in Los Angeles, California, it created more than 3,000 jobs and brought in more than $160 million across local businesses.

An average of 72,500 people saw each show on The Eras Tour.

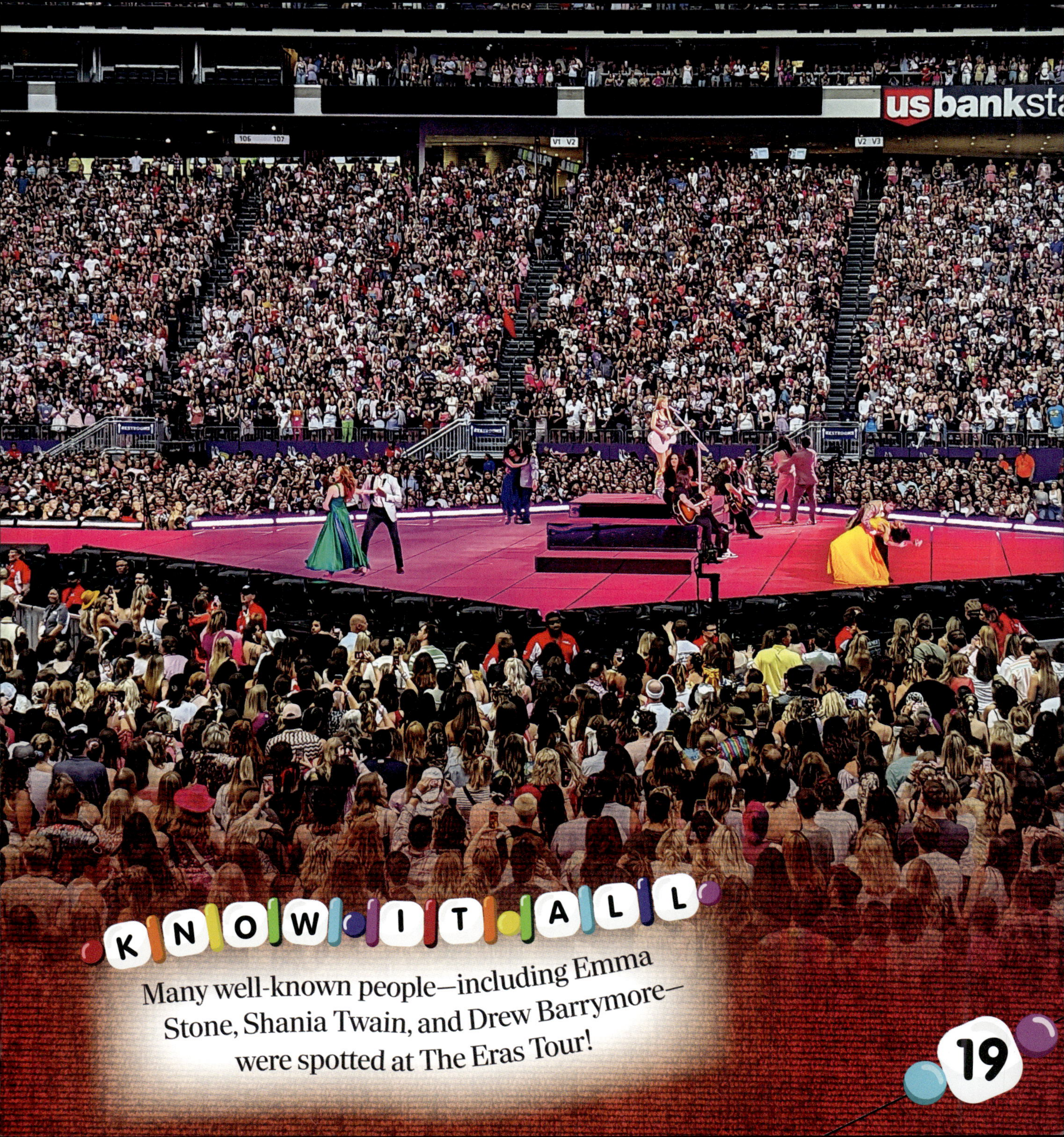

KNOW IT ALL

Many well-known people—including Emma Stone, Shania Twain, and Drew Barrymore—were spotted at The Eras Tour!

Cities were happy to be a stop on The Eras Tour—and to get the extra money it brought in. Some places changed the name of streets or the city itself to have to do with Taylor for a day or two. Minneapolis, Minnesota, changed its name to Swiftieapolis for one day!

Even the United States economy felt the Taylor Swift Effect during The Eras Tour. After the first 53 stops of the tour, the **gross domestic product (GDP)** of the country rose about $4.3 billion!

KNOW IT ALL

A movie of The Eras Tour called *Taylor Swift: The Eras Tour* came out in 2023. It brought in over $260 million worldwide. It broke the record for the most money earned by a concert movie.

When *Taylor Swift: The Eras Tour* came out on Disney+, it had over 4 million views in three days. This broke the record for the most streams of a music movie on Disney+.

HOW SWIFTIES LISTEN

Today, most people use streaming services to listen to music. Artists don't sell as many CDs or **vinyl** records as they used to—unless they're Taylor Swift. Her fans buy her albums on CD and vinyl to collect the different cover art or hear bonus songs.

In fact, fans have bought Taylor's vinyl records in such huge numbers that she is said to be helping make vinyl popular again. In 2023, her albums made up nearly 6.5 percent of all vinyl record sales in the United States!

The album *1989 (Taylor's Version)* was the only vinyl album to sell more than 1 million copies worldwide in 2023!

KNOW IT ALL

When sales of all the Taylor Swift albums available on vinyl are added together, she sold more than 3.4 million vinyl records in the United States in 2023.

FOOTBALL SWIFTIES

In 2023, it came out that Taylor had started dating Travis Kelce, a National Football League (NFL) player on the Kansas City Chiefs team. She went to some of his games to cheer him on. Swifties started watching football games just to try and see Taylor in the stands! After the first game Taylor attended, more than 2 million more female viewers tuned in for the next one.

Swifties started to support the Kansas City Chiefs too. Sales of **merchandise** with the team's name and logo tripled, especially jerseys with Travis's number, 87.

IN TAYLOR'S WORDS

"Football is awesome it turns out. I've been missing out my whole life."
(*Time*, December 6, 2023)

The first time Taylor went to a Chiefs game was in September 2023. After that, the NFL reported the Chiefs had broken the record for the number of merchandise purchases for one team in one day!

POP CULTURE ICON

Taylor has connected with millions of fans around the world since her first album was released in 2006. For almost 20 years, she has worked to make changes in the music industry. She has inspired many artists to start making music too. In addition, Taylor speaks up for herself and others, firing up her fans to learn about politics and pop culture.

Taylor has impacted so many parts of pop culture—and beyond. It's likely we will continue to see the Taylor Swift Effect for years to come!

KNOW IT ALL

The Taylor Swift Effect is a popular topic. Schools, including Harvard University, have classes where students can learn about her career, songwriting, and pop culture impact.

THROUGHOUT HER CAREER, TAYLOR HAS WON A LOT OF AWARDS FOR HER IMPACT ON THE MUSIC INDUSTRY AND POPULAR CULTURE, INCLUDING:

- 2011 – WOMAN OF THE YEAR, *BILLBOARD*
- 2014 – WOMAN OF THE YEAR, *BILLBOARD*
- 2019 - WOMAN OF THE DECADE, *BILLBOARD*
- 2023 – INNOVATOR OF THE YEAR, IHEART RADIO
- 2023 – PERSON OF THE YEAR, *TIME*

Taylor gave a long interview with *Time* magazine when she was named Person of the Year in 2023. She talks about her life, career, and the people who inspire her.

ACTIVITY: TEST YOUR KNOWLEDGE!

Are you the ultimate Taylor Swift fan? Answer these questions and check your answers at the bottom of page 29!

1

WHAT YEAR WAS TAYLOR SWIFT BORN?

A. 1989 B. 1990
C. 1987 D. 1992

2

WHEN DID TAYLOR START PLAYING GUITAR?

A. AGE 10 B. AGE 16
C. AGE 20 D. AGE 12

3

WHICH TAYLOR SWIFT SONG IS ABOUT HOW MEN AND WOMEN ARE TREATED DIFFERENTLY?

A. "YOU NEED TO CALM DOWN"
B. "BETTY"
C. "BEJEWELED"
D. "THE MAN"

4

WHAT COLOR LIPSTICK DOES TAYLOR USUALLY WEAR?

A. PINK
B. PURPLE
C. RED
D. MAROON

5

WHAT WAS TAYLOR'S 2023–2024 TOUR CALLED?

A. THE ERAS TOUR
B. ALL MY MUSIC TOUR
C. THE MIDNIGHTS TOUR
D. LOVER FEST

6

WHAT WAS TAYLOR'S FIRST ALBUM CALLED?

A. *SPEAK NOW*
B. *TAYLOR SWIFT*
C. *MIDNIGHTS*
D. *FOLKLORE*

ANSWER KEY
1. A; 2. D; 3. D; 4. C; 5. A; 6. B

GLOSSARY

candidate: Someone running for a government office.

career: The job someone chooses to do for a long time.

genre: A kind of music.

gross domestic product (GDP): The value of the goods and services produced by those living in a nation during a year all added together.

impact: Strong effect.

inspire: To cause someone to want to do something.

LGBTQ+: Stands for the lesbian, gay, bisexual, transgender, and queer or questioning community.

master recording: The official, original recording of a song. It is sometimes just called a master.

merchandise: Goods sold such as clothing or posters.

politics: The activities of the government and officials.

rare: Uncommon or special.

social media: Websites and apps that allow people to communicate with one another.

stream: To transfer data in a continuous way, meant to be watched or listened to immediately.

version: A form of something that is different from others.

vinyl: A kind of plastic used to make records.

FOR MORE INFORMATION

Books

Anderson, Kirsten. *Who Is Taylor Swift?* New York, New York: Penguin Workshop, 2024.

Kawa, Katie. *Taylor Swift: Making a Difference as a Songwriter.* New York, New York: KidHaven Publishing, 2022.

Websites

Taylor Swift
www.taylorswift.com/
Read more about Taylor and her work on her official website.

Universal Music Publishing Group: Taylor Swift
www.umusicpub.com/us/Artists/T/Taylor-Swift
Learn about Taylor's recent songs and albums on her record label's website.

Publisher's note to educators and parents: Our editors have carefully reviewed these websites to ensure that they are suitable for students. Many websites change frequently, however, and we cannot guarantee that a site's future contents will continue to meet our high standards of quality and educational value. Be advised that students should be closely supervised whenever they access the internet.

INDEX